Busy Toddler, Happy Mom

Over 280 Activities to Engage Your
Toddler in Small Motor and Gross
Motor Activities, Crafts, Language
Development and Sensory Play

Gayle Jervis & Kristen Jervis Cacka

DEDICATION

For the Special Little People in our lives,
J, V &M!

CONTENTS

DISCLAIMER

The authors and the publisher cannot be held responsible for damage, mishap, injury incurred during the use of or because of activities in this book. Appropriate and reasonable caution and adult supervision of children involved in activities and corresponding to the age and capability of each child involved is recommended at all times. Do not leave children unattended at any time. Observe safety and caution at all times. While all attempts have been made to provide effective, verifiable information in this book, neither the author nor publisher assumes responsibility for errors, inaccuracies or omissions.

INTRODUCTION

Do you often wish you had more ideas on how to keep your child stimulated at home? Do you find yourself signing up for expensive toddler programs since they give you the confidence that you have provided all that your toddler needs for his developmental growth? Do you wish that your toddler could be more fully engaged in his play so that you have time to do the laundry? Have you purchased activity books to give you more ideas on how to entertain your toddler to discover that they are more appropriate for groups of toddlers at a daycare or for a specialized program?

As a Grandma who enjoys planning

activities for my grandchildren, I was frustrated when I couldn't find an easy to implement program for my two toddler grandchildren. My daughter was even more frustrated since as a busy mom she wanted to implement a program for her little girl, but one that was affordable and had easy to find supplies. We also knew that we wanted a book with specific objectives so that we could enjoy watching these toddlers develop specific skills. Of course, we also wanted to ensure that these activities provided many opportunities not just to stimulate our toddlers but to increase the fun interactions between grandparent/parent and child.

You may be wondering what specific skills are necessary to develop in your little person who already has made significant developments without a formal program. Admittedly, the skills we will mention are developed at least to some extent without intention. And yet, if you converse with a kindergarten teacher, you will quickly learn that some of those same skills haven't been developed to the extent that they need when they begin kindergarten. For example, it is common for children to enter kindergarten unable to hold a pencil properly since they have not sufficiently developed their small motor skills. Other children who may have been happiest when they were coloring may be lacking those larger muscles in their arms and legs in order to run and keep up with the other children.

Therefore, this book has been divided into specific chapters that work on specific skills: small motor skills, gross motor skills, arts and crafts, sensory abilities, books and language development. As these activities are introduced, you are also increasing your toddler's math and reading readiness, her vocabulary, her understanding of language, and her understanding of her world.

As you look through these activities, you will gravitate toward certain chapters since they are more in keeping with your own temperament. That is why we encourage you to do activities from each chapter to permit a balanced scope and sequence of activities for your child. As you continue to look through these activities, you will also come to the same conclusion that we did: learning is neither linear nor isolated. For example, when your toddler is engaged in a sensory activity, she is not only enjoying the sense of touch, smell and so on, but she is most likely developing fine motor skills. As she is doing an activity as follow up to a book you have read to her, she is not only developing more vocabulary and understanding of her world, she may be performing a gross motor activity of running like a bear.

You may be wondering if all of these activities are going to reduce even more of your time since you imagine your toddler never playing with his toys! Actually, you gain more time for yourself as you give her more ideas for independent play. For example, in one of the activities, you may have shown her how to have a pretend tea party. The next day, she will most likely surprise you by repeating this activity alone. Also, you will be surprised how often after a one on one session with you, your child will be ready to return to his independent play.

You may have one further hesitation about this program if you have more than one child. How can you spend time with your toddler when your preschooler is also demanding attention? When I home schooled my two children, I often gave some independent activity to my daughter while I gave some one on one attention to her older brother's activity. And then I would switch in order to give my daughter my full attention. Often that became a win-win situation since it gave my older son undistracted time to work on his Lego without that constant interruption from his inquisitive sister! Other times my two children enjoyed doing the same activity together that merely required higher expectations for my older son. My only caution when you include both children is to make sure that your oldest doesn't dominate the activity. Your toddler learns best when he receives face-to-face, one-on-one interactions and he may resort to being just an observer when there is competition from his older sibling.

Before you start this program, please continue reading the following description of what the objectives are for each chapter and also read the suggested plan how to implement the activities.

AN OVERVIEW OF OBJECTIVES

Most people agree that toddlerhood starts at 18 months and ends at three years old. That spread in time is a huge span of developmental growth. Therefore, if you are starting this book when your child is 18 months, please don't be frustrated when he doesn't seem to comprehend how to do a particular activity. Also, don't frustrate your child by insisting that he excels at the activity because you know of another toddler who quite easily does it. Your role is merely to introduce these activities in order to stimulate his development and on his own time, he will perform the activity really well. You will merely repeat the exercise perhaps a month later to see whether he is ready to try it.

As already mentioned, this book contains the following chapter titles: Small Motor Activities, Gross Motor Activities, Arts and Crafts, Sensory Activities, Books to Read and Language Development. Below you will find the specific objectives that are being targeted in each chapter.

SMALL MOTOR ACTIVITIES:

In the chapter called Small Motor Activities, you are giving her activities that will help her develop muscles to increase her dexterity, which will enable her to write and to grasp small objects. Without the development of these muscles, she will have difficulty using scissors, playing the piano and anything else that requires precise hand and finger movements. She will be developing the strength of her hands and wrists when you give her the opportunity to squeeze and roll out play dough and when she is crumpling paper for a collage. In this chapter, your child may find some of the activities are challenging since they will eventually require her to demonstrate some of this growing strength as she use tongs, tweezers and eventually scissors.

GROSS MOTOR ACTIVITIES:

Gross motor skills involve movements using the large muscles of the body. They include things like running, jumping, catching and throwing balls, and other large muscle activities. Whenever the weather permits you to do these activities outside, there are added benefits as your child has more room to move, and of course he will get his much needed Vitamin D!

ARTS AND CRAFTS:

In this chapter on arts and crafts, your child is being given more opportunities to have sensory experiences while at the same time developing his small motor skills as he holds crayons, markers, and paint brushes. The emphasis during these activities is process not product.

SENSORY ACTIVITIES:

When you think of sensory activities, you may immediately think of children playing with sand or water or finger paint. Certainly you will be giving her many opportunities to develop her sense of touch, but often other senses are being engaged also. If she is finger painting with shaving cream or chocolate pudding, her sense of smell is being exercised. And when you give her permission to lick her fingers, her sense of taste is being exercised.

Besides providing fun for your child, is there any other reason why your child does these activities? First, you are allowing him to assume the role of scientist as he observes an ice cube melting and returning to its original form of water. Second, you are preparing him for math as he pours water into a large cup and then takes that cup and pours water into two smaller cups. In this chapter, you have a potpourri of activities that will exercise your child's sensory muscles as a means to keep his brain healthy while he has many wonderful self-discoveries.

BOOKS TO READ:

You cannot read too many books to your toddler! Sadly, many parents only read to their children before they tuck them into bed. Every time you read a book to your child, you are giving her opportunities to hear new words and to observe something new about her world.

Therefore, choose well written books filled with pages of interesting illustrations. You can find such books by choosing books from authors who have reviewed toddler books and recommend the best. Perhaps, consider purchasing one of the following books: <u>Books for Babies and Toddlers</u> by Kathleen Odean or <u>Babies Need Books</u> by Dorothy Butler.

Besides your reading a variety of books each day, we have chosen in this chapter specific books that include various activities to help him better understand the story and to better understand his world. There will be an emphasis on teaching him how to pretend play so that he is developing his imagination.

LANGUAGE DEVELOPMENT:

Your child is learning new words at an

exponential rate. Her level of comprehension is greater than what she can verbalize. Therefore, talk to her continually as you go about your daily routine. When you are cooking, explain what you are doing, what ingredients you are putting in the bowl, what pots and bowls you are using. The exercises in this chapter will give you ideas on how to introduce to her even more vocabulary words.

Please keep these mini-lessons short and enjoyable and do not get frustrated when he doesn't want to learn what you are teaching him!! If you are continually talking to him and reading to him, your child's language development just comes naturally. These activities merely supplement this natural development and bring to his attention some specific words and concepts.

Activities in this chapter have been designed to introduce and increase your child's understanding of various language concepts. Of course, these activities also provide more opportunities for conversation between the two of you. Through these activities, she is also introduced to many math concepts such as big, small, tall, long, light, heavy, and so on.

HOW TO PLAN
YOUR ACTIVITIES

Some of you will be tempted to see this book as a potpourri of ideas that you can indiscriminately choose from. However, the weakness to this approach is of course you're not giving your child a balance of a variety of activities that focus on different developmental skills. Therefore, we encourage you to choose an activity from each chapter for each week to remedy that weakness.

As you choose the activities for the week, you will want to check your calendar to determine how many activities will be appropriate for the week. If you are home all week, you will most likely choose more activities than during a week that is filled with various appointments.

As you choose your activities, remember that children thrive on repetition. You may decide to rotate your activities every other day just to give your child variety. However, you may discover that there is one activity that your child really enjoys and you will repeat it every day. When you choose an activity from Books to Read, you may decide to just read that one picture book every day and only do its activity once or twice a week. Of course, that is assuming that you are reading many other picture books to your child.

When you have chosen the activities for the week, make sure you have all of the supplies. In fact, collect your supplies for the week and put them all in a container for easy access.

Either post on your fridge or keep in your storage container a sheet of paper where you have written the names of the chapters. Beside each chapter name, write the numbers of the activities that you are planning on doing so that you can easily find them. When you begin doing these activities with your child, please remember that they require your adult supervision. You know your child best. If your child still puts things into his mouth, you may decide he is not ready for certain activities.

Before you begin choosing activities, refer to the chapter on Supplies since you may want to have a basic list of supplies so that you only need to occasionally find a specific item for an activity. Also, in this chapter, there is extra information about optional purchases such as a flannel board or ideas on how to make your own flannel board.

Besides being an educator and a former home schooling mom, I am a Grandma who sees my two toddler grandchildren at least once a week. I want them to be excited coming to my place and these activities give us many opportunities to enjoy one another. My daughter, who is co-author of this book, pulls from these activities every day to ensure that her little girl is receiving the necessary stimulation.

May these activities give you as much enjoyment as they do for my daughter and me when we are interacting with our little people.

CHAPTER 1:

SMALL MOTOR ACTIVITIES

The following activities are helping your toddler to develop muscles that will help with his dexterity which enable him to write and to grasp any small object. Many of these activities can be repeated throughout the year so you may want to keep the specific supplies for those activities together in a bag and label them. Remember that toddlers love repetition.

IMPORTANT: Close Adult Supervision is Required with Each of These Activities

1. Give your toddler some large tubular pasta and a shoelace. Show her how to thread the shoelace through the pasta.

2. Take an empty long wrapping paper tube and place one end on the edge of the sofa and the other end on the floor. Give him a small ball such as a Ping Pong ball to roll down the tube.

3. Give her some individually wrapped toilet tissues, some boxes of facial tissue or some small tins of food such as tomato paste. Then let her have fun stacking them.

4. Wrap a small toy and discuss what might be inside it. Give it to him to unwrap. Then rewrap as he watches. Have him unwrap it again.

5. Cut such fruits as strawberries and bananas into chunks. Show her how to slide the chunks onto a long plastic straw. Then show her how you can take off one chunk at a time, dip it into some yogurt and eat it.

6. Place a paper towel over a water-filled glass. Wrap a rubber band around the top of the glass to hold the towel in place. Then place a penny on top of the paper towel in the center of the glass. Give your child a pencil to poke holes in the towel until the penny sinks to the bottom of the glass.

7. You will need a small sheet of coarse sandpaper and various lengths of chunky wool. Show him how to place these lengths of wool on the sandpaper and how the strands stick to it.

8. Use a large photo or picture and laminate it or put it between the sheets of clear contact paper. Cut it into several pieces to create a puzzle.

9. Give her two glasses, one empty and one filled with water. Then show her how to use a large eyedropper in order to transfer some of the water into the empty glass.

10. Tie the ends or corners of several scarves together. Stuff the scarf inside an empty baby wipes container and pull a small portion up through the lid and then close the lid. Let your toddler enjoy pulling the scarf out of the container.

11. Give your child some magnets to put on a cookie sheet. As your child puts the magnets on the cookie sheet and takes them off, talk about the magnets' colors, sizes, etc.

12. Use two matching sets of stickers. Put a few in a line on a page and see if he can match the pattern. Initially, you may need to lift an edge of the sticker off the page since that can be difficult to do.

13. You will need a piece of thin Styrofoam or craft foam and a few cookie cutters. Cut out shapes in the Styrofoam with the cookie cutters and yet still keep the frame of the Styrofoam intact. See if your child

can place the cookie cutters back into their appropriate holes.

14. Give her a collection of pompoms that vary in color and size and see if she can sort them by color or size into several small dishes. For younger toddlers, put a sample pompom color in each dish.

15. Gather a selection of primary color paint chips or cut squares of card stock or construction paper. Make sure you have several of the same color. Choose primary colors. See if he can match the colors. Initially, he may be just content to play with the colored chips stacking them or making patterns with them.

16. Use a colander that has fairly large holes and give her some pipe cleaners. Show her how to put the pipe cleaners through the holes of the colander.

17. Choose a variety of objects such as a key, a cookie cutter, a spoon, a child's scissors and a pencil. Then trace these objects on separate pieces of paper. Put those traced objects into a box such as a photo box or shoebox. Place the sheets of paper on the table and then give him the box of items. Show him how to take an object out of the box and match it to the sheets of paper.

VARIATION: Spread the sheets on the floor where he must find the appropriate match.

18. Give your child several disposable cups and show her how to stack them together and take them apart.

VARIATION: If the cups are different colors, can she stack them according to color? If they are Styrofoam cups, use some colored markers and color their rims different colors in order to sort them by color.

19. Tape a sheet of paper to your table. Let him choose a crayon to make some marks on the page. Take a crayon and make some straight or wavy lines and tell him what kind of line you drew. See if he will copy your lines.

20. Put some Velcro dots on small toys such as building blocks. Show her how she can take one of the blocks and make it stick to another block.

21. Give him a piece of Styrofoam, a plastic hammer and some golf tees. Show him how to hammer tees into the Styrofoam.

22. Fill an ice cube tray with water and some food coloring. When the ice cubes are frozen, fill a plastic bowl with water. Drop the ice cubes into the water. Give your child a large spoon or tongs to scoop out the ice cubes into an empty bowl to watch them melt. Talk about the word "frozen" and "melt".

23. Cut various colors of construction paper into squares. Then take some wooden clothes pegs and with a marker, color the tops of them with colors matching the construction paper. See if she can match the pegs with the paper. Can she squeeze the clothes peg open and place inside it the piece of construction paper?

24. Give him a tote bag and see if he can open and close the zipper. Inside the tote bag, put one of his onesies or something else that has snaps to show him how to use them. Also, include a cardigan or shirt that has large buttons and large buttonholes to show him how to work them.

25. Fill one deep container with some water. Give your child a turkey baster and show her how to squeeze and release the baster to get some water to rise up into the baster. Then show her how to release water into an empty bowl.

26. Stack six disposable cups in a triangle on the floor. Show your child how to roll a small ball and knock down the cups. Have him start close enough so that he has success. Then gradually have him step a little further back.

27. Give your child a small container of pennies and a piggy bank. She will enjoy putting the pennies in the piggy bank's narrow coin slot.

28. Put some small pieces of tissue paper on a plate. Then give him a clothes peg to pick up the small pieces and to put them on another plate. To help him properly use the clothes peg, it may help to put a single dot on one side of a clothes peg and two dots on the other side. Then you can show your child how to place his thumb on the one dot and two fingers on the other side.

29. Give your child a selection of shoes and boots to sort. As she puts the appropriate pairs together, talk about when you wear various shoes and boots and whom they belong to.

30. Cut out five circles and five squares from flannel. Place them on your flannel board and have her take off only the circles. If you don't have a flannel board, just cut the shapes from construction paper and lay these shapes on the table. Have him find only circles.

31. Give your child a plastic container and some clothes pegs. Show her how to attach clothes pegs around the edge of the entire container.

32. Give your child a magnifying glass and wander through your house looking more closely at various items such as leaves on a plant, a toy, food etc. This activity works really well if you can go outside and look

more closely at rocks, pinecones, insects and leaves.

33. You will need a muffin tin, a pair of tweezers, small pompoms and cotton balls. Show your toddler how to pick up these small items with tweezers and put them into the muffin tin.

VARIATION: Separate the pompoms by color.

34. You will need two empty cardboard paper towel tubes. Cut them into 1.5" circles that your toddler can thread with a long piece of ribbon or shoelace. Tie one of the circles at the end of the shoelace so the threaded circles don't fall off.

35. Give your child a large lump of play dough and stick a long piece of spaghetti into it. Then give your toddler a small dish of cheerios or any other cereal that has a hole in it. Show him how to take the strand of

spaghetti and slip a piece of cereal onto it.

36. Take a large piece of play dough and hide small objects inside the "sculpture." Hide such items as buttons and coins. She could use tweezers to find these items.

37. Give your child some thick elastic bands, or ponytail holders and a plastic cup. Show him how to stretch the elastic around the cup.

38. Give your child some play dough and plastic cookie cutters. The purchased play dough is not that easy to manipulate. You might like to try the following play dough recipe:

> 1 cup white flour
> 1/4 cup of salt
> 2 tsps cream of tartar
> 1 cup water
> 1 tbsp oil
> 2 tsps food coloring

Mix flour, salt, and cream of tartar in a saucepan. Add the remaining ingredients and cook over medium heat. When the mixture forms a ball, take it out of the saucepan and knead on a slightly floured surface. Store in an airtight container or plastic bag. To help this play dough last longer, store in the fridge.

39. Choose paint chips with the same color but that vary in tone. Take doubles of each. At home, cut these paint chips apart. Now see if your child notices whether the paint chips you show her are the same color but are different tones. See if she can sort them.

40. Make a clothesline by tying some string from one chair to another. You can use color chips from a hardware store or doll clothes or even your child's socks for him to hang up with clothes pegs.

41. Put some dried beans such as lima or kidney beans into a deep and large bowl. Give your child a small ladle or scoop to pour the beans into another bowl. When beans fall out of the bowl, encourage her to put them back into the bowl.

As with each activity listed, only you can determine whether your child is developmentally ready to try it. The next few exercises using a child's scissors will especially require your discernment:

42. With a child's plastic scissors, you can show him how to use them to cut long thin rolls of play dough.

43. When your child uses scissors well with play dough, she may be ready to cut taut lengths of wool. You can tape some lengths of wool tightly across the top of a baking dish.

44. After much practice with scissors cutting long thin rolls of play dough and cutting lengths of wool, you may want to see how he does cutting paper. Initially, hold the paper tightly for him to help facilitate his cutting it. Eventually, allow him to cut the paper without your help.

Gayle Jervis & Kristen Jervis Cacka

CHAPTER 2:

GROSS MOTOR ACTIVITIES

Gayle Jervis & Kristen Jervis Cacka

Gross motor skills involve movements using the large muscles of the body. They include things like running, jumping, catching and throwing balls, and other large muscle activities. Developing these movements develop control of the arms and legs and even smaller movements of the hands and fingers.

IMPORTANT: Close Adult Supervision is Required with Each of These Activities.

1. Sit on the floor across from your child with your legs spread. Roll a ball back and forth to one another.

2. Put a box on its side and roll the ball into the box.

3. Place a beanbag on her back while she is crawling on the floor. See if she can crawl around the room without the beanbag falling off.

4. Line up several empty plastic soda bottles or unused paper towel rolls. Give him a large ball to knock them over.

5. Attach the end of a paint stir stick to the back of a firm paper plate with masking tape. Throw a balloon up in the air and see if she can catch the balloon on the plate. She can also bat the balloon around the room with her "paper plate bat."

6. Create a line on the floor with masking tape. Can she walk on the line? Can she jump up and down along the line? Can she walk the line with a beanbag on top of her head?

7. Hold a yardstick or dowel rod at various heights and have your toddler jump over it. Have him crawl under it or walk around it. Through this exercise, he also learns what it means to go under, go over and go around.

8. Lie on the floor together and do some yoga poses. Do the fun ones such as the Downward Facing Dog, the Cobra or the Cat. Check youtube.com if you need to know what these positions look like.

9. Hold hands and walk in a circle while singing the following verse. And of course, fall down as you sing the last line!

> Ring around the Rosie
> A pocket full of posies
> A-tishoo! A-tishoo!
> We all fall down.

10. Place a pile of pillows on the floor. Show her how to take a running start and jump into the pile.

11. Take some plastic eggs and fill them with small treats and then hide them in a room. Let her enjoy finding them and eating her treat.

12. Hide your child's plush animals in a darkened room. Give her a flashlight to go hunting for her animals.

    VARIATION: Go for a short walk outside when it is getting dark so that she can enjoy using her small flashlight.

13. Make some maracas by putting rice or dried beans into a small container that has a secure lid. Pringles containers or similar containers that hold toddler snacks in them work well. Put some packing tape around the lid so that your toddler cannot open it. Play some uplifting music and

dance around the room shaking your maracas.

14. Make some tambourines by putting some dried beans onto one small foil pan. Take another foil pan and staple together. Tape over the staples. Play some uplifting music and shake your tambourines. He will enjoy dancing much more if you participate!

15. Play some music and dance, but when the music stops, fall down or "Freeze" in one position.

16. Sit across from your child with legs close enough to one another that you can hold each other's hands. Rock back and forth holding your child's hands singing:

> Row, Row, Row your Boat,
> Gently Down the Stream.
> Merrily, Merrily, Merrily,
> Life is but a Dream.

17. Slide some jingle bells onto a length of narrow elastic or ribbon. Tie the ends together and then slide the bracelet onto his wrist. Encourage him to dance while he enjoys shaking his hand to make the bells jingle.

18. Create a string trail throughout some rooms by securing the string on the floor with masking tape. Place a toy or snack at the end of the string trail for her to find.

19. Give him two spoons to strike together while you play some music.

20. Create 2 megaphones by rolling a sheet of paper into a cone and taping the ends. Then begin speaking loudly through your megaphone to your child. "Hello, hello, how are you?" See if she will imitate what you are doing. Walk through the house experimenting with the volume and sounds you can make using your megaphone.

21. Play a game of taking giant steps and then taking very short steps through out the room.

22. March around reciting "The Grand Old Duke of York". If you aren't familiar with the following verse, just write it out on an index card and carry it when you are marching. When you march up the hill, throw your hands up high and when you are going down the hill, march as low as you can go.

> The grand old Duke of York
> He had 10,000 men
> He marched them up the hill
> And then he marched them down again
> And when you're up, you're up
> And when you're down, you're down
> And when you're only halfway up
> You're neither up
> Nor down.

23. Let your toddler try walking in some of your flat shoes. He actually develops balance as he tries to walk in larger shoes.

24. If you have an exercise ball, sit on the ball while you are holding her and roll back and forth on the ball and then sideways. Then seat her on the ball and as you hold her up, rock her back and forth and then sideways. Show her how to lie on her tummy on the exercise ball.

25. Make a square with masking tape on the floor, or put a small blanket on the floor and show your child how to jump in and out of the square.

26. Sing the song, "Head and Shoulders, Knees and Toes" and do the appropriate motions. Have fun with this song by singing it faster each time you sing it. You can do this activity with your young toddler, but since he is just learning the parts of his body, don't expect too much

accuracy or speed from him.

> Head, shoulders, knees and toes,
> Knees and toes.
> Head, shoulders, knees and toes,
> Knees and toes.
> Eyes and ears and mouth and nose

27. Hold hands and while you walk in a circle, sing the traditional song, "Here We Go Looby Loo." At the end of the song, jump up with arms extended

> Here we go looby loo,
> Here we go looby li,
> Here we go looby loo,
> All on a Saturday night.

28. Sing the song, "Pop Goes the Weasel" as you walk in a circle holding hands. At the end of the song, jump up, and then fall to the ground.

> All around the cobbler's bench,
> The monkey chased the weasel
> The monkey thought it was all in fun
> POP goes the weasel.

29. Do the appropriate motions to the
    following rhyme, "Teddy Bear, Teddy
    Bear":

    Teddy bear, teddy bear, turn around
    Teddy bear, teddy bear, touch the ground.
    Teddy bear, teddy bear, show your shoe
    Teddy bear, teddy bear, crawl right
    through.
    (Have your child crawl between your legs)

30. Use a shower curtain ring or binder ring to
    attach some strips of ribbon. She can
    swing them from side to side and up and
    down as you play some uplifting music.

31. Hold hands and walk in a circle as you sing
    the following chorus. When you sing the
    verse, stop and do the appropriate
    motions:

    Here we go round the mulberry bush,
    the mulberry bush, the mulberry bush
    Here we go round the mulberry bush,
    so early in the morning.

This is the way we clap our hands,
clap our hands, clap our hands,
This is the way we clap our hands, so
early in the morning.

This is the way we stamp our feet . . .
This is the way we turn around . . .
This is the way we reach and stretch. . .
This is the way we sit right down. . .
This is the way we wash our face. . . .

32. Give your child a large spoon and a plastic
egg. Now see how far he can carry this egg
on top of the spoon without dropping it.

VARIATION: Show him how to get on
his hands and knees and push the plastic
egg using only his nose.

33. Give your child a ball and show her how
to kick it across the room or kick the ball
outside in the backyard. See if you can kick
the ball back and forth to each other.

34. Show your toddler how to kick a ball or a beanbag up in the air. This activity works really well outside.

35. Play the music for the "Chicken Dance" and have fun doing this dance together.

36. Use a yardstick or dowel and show him how to limbo. Play the appropriate music, "Let's Do The Limbo" by Chubby Checker!

37. Dance to some disco music with your toddler. For extra fun, darken your room and give her a flashlight to use while the two of you twirl around the room to such oldies as "Dancing Queen" by Abba or "I Will Survive" by Gloria Gaynor.

38. Play "The Twist" by Chubby Checker and show your toddler how to twist!

39. Give your child a child-sized mop to sweep the floor. Some handles on adult

sized mops can be shortened for a child to manage.

40. Play some Hawaiian music and show your child how to sway his arms and hips to the music.

41. Place a rope on the floor and have her jump over it. Then start wiggling the rope and encourage her to keep jumping over it.

42. Give your toddler a large cardboard box to push around the room. Then put a hole in the side of the box and tie a small rope through the hole. Now have your toddler pull the box around the room. Give him some small items to put in the box and have him pull it around the room. This activity also works well outside.

43. Encourage your child to use a riding toy, since this activity will strengthen her legs.

44. Create a tunnel for your child to crawl through by placing a blanket over a table and some kitchen chairs.

45. Crawl on the floor. Pretend you are various animals and make the appropriate sounds!

46. Show your child how to walk backwards. Make sure he doesn't run into anything! Play outside where you have lots of room.

47. Gather together all of your pillows and help your toddler build a hill. Place a blanket over all of the pillows. Let her enjoy climbing her hill, jumping off her hill, etc.

48. Give your child two empty tissue boxes. Show him how he can put his feet inside them and walk across the room.

49. Place suction cups on a mirror or window and have your toddler pull them off. Then place them a little higher so that she will have to go up on her toes in order to reach them and pull them off. Now place the suction cups even a little higher so that your toddler will have to jump up in order to reach them and pull them off.

Gayle Jervis & Kristen Jervis Cacka

CHAPTER 3:

ARTS AND CRAFTS

Some Tips Before You Begin Arts and Crafts with Your Child:

Arts and crafts can be messy so make sure your floor is covered with a plastic tablecloth. Also, give your child an art smock or an old shirt to wear.

Most of the projects that your toddler does could be used as cards for her to give to family and friends. You just have to add a greeting.

The most important thing for you to remember is that your toddler is more interested in the process than the product and this fact can be difficult for adults who focus more naturally on results.

Even though your toddler's joy comes from the process and not from the product, she may still enjoy your finding a place to display some of her work. To make it even more special, purchase a few cheap frames and regularly rotate and frame her work.

It's impossible to keep all of her projects, but you can take a photo of her and her work before trashing it! It is good to keep some of her projects or at least take photos of them, so that by the time she turns three, you could compare her work from the beginning of the year to the end of the year.

Many of these projects can be used to depict various seasons or celebrations by choosing appropriate colors or items. For example, use heart shaped cookie cutters to dip into red paint for Valentines Day.

Finally, many of these activities mention that you need paper. However, remember that you can use cardboard, Styrofoam, wrapping paper, paper plates or anything else that you have at home.

IMPORTANT: Close Adult Supervision is Required with Each of These Activities

1. Give your child a sheet of construction paper and some chalk. When he is finished putting his chalk marks on the paper, you can spray the paper with hair spray to set the chalk.

2. Wet some construction paper with a damp sponge and draw on the wet paper with chalk.

3. Give your child some non-toxic and washable markers to draw on a paper towel or coffee filter. The absorbency of the paper will make the colors blur.

4. Draw a shape with a thick black marker on a piece of paper towel. Give her a brush and water to paint on the towel.

5. Crumple some newspaper into a ball and dip in liquid paint. Press the ball all over some heavy plain paper. Use a different ball of newspaper for each paint color.

6. Mix some food coloring with water and pour into an ice cube tray. When close to frozen, insert craft sticks into some of the cubes. Then give your toddler an "ice popsicle" to paint with.

7. Place one of the sheets from a "Paint With Water" book into a light, shallow baking dish. Sprinkle a little powdered paint onto the paper. Then place an ice cube on top of the sheet. Give your child the container to rotate to make a painting.

8. Mix a little bit of glue with liquid paint. Give your child a feather to use as a brush and paint the mixture onto the paper. Then glue on a few feathers.

9. Using an old salad spinner, remove the plastic insert and place a small paper plate or coffee filter on the bottom. Then replace the insert back into the bowl. Dribble some liquid paint onto the spinner, put the lid on and show your toddler how to spin it. When he is finished, take out the paper and show him what he made.

10. Cut a piece of paper to fill the bottom of a small shoebox or an empty baby wipe container. Pour a small amount of paint into a dish and dip a rock into the paint. Place the rock into the container and shut the lid. Shake the box up and down and side to side. Open the lid and look at the design the rock has made.

11. Pry the top off an empty roll-on deodorant or shoe polish bottle. Fill it with liquid paint. Now snap the top back onto the bottle. Give her the bottle and a sheet of paper to paint.

12. Beat together ½ cup cold water and 1 cup powdered laundry soap until stiff. Then add some food coloring. Have your child dip her paintbrush in the mixture and begin to paint.

13. Pour a small amount of paint into a shallow container that will be big enough to dip the wheels of a small toy car. Place the car into this paint and have your child roll it back and forth a few times so that the wheels are well covered with paint. Then show him how to roll the car across a large sheet of paper to make tire tracks. For less mess, you might decide to get the car wheels wet with paint and then give him the painted car to drive across a large sheet of paper.

14. Pour a small amount of paint into a container big enough to dip different sizes of building blocks. Dip each block into the paint and use them to make prints on a sheet of paper.

15. Mix some salt or sand with powdered paint and put into a shaker type container, such as a salt shaker, one for each color. Brush white liquid glue onto a sheet of paper with a small brush or dribble it on with a spoon. You may want to do this first step. Then give your toddler the salt shaker with the tempera paint powder mixture and sprinkle over the glue. When the glue is dry, shake off the excess powder.

16. Place a plastic container upside down. Cut various lengths of tape and place them around the edge of the container. Use a variety of different types of tape and different colors such as masking tape, painter's tape and clear tape. Have your toddler pull off these lengths from the container and stick onto a sheet of construction paper to create a collage.

17. Give your toddler a paper plate, a rock or a small empty bottle to put stickers on it.

18. Cut a raw potato in half, dip into the paint and make a print on the construction paper. You can also cut out a design into the raw potato. Or cut an apple in half to use as her stamp.

19. Pour liquid paint into a shallow tray. Give your toddler a variety of cookie cutters to dip in the paint to make prints on the paper.

20. Drop thick blobs of liquid paint on one side of a sheet of folded paper. Show your child how to press the paper together and create a design.

21. Dip a small paint roller into paint. Show him how to roll the paint on the paper.

22. Let her enjoy the wonder of creating new colors. Give her two colors to paint with such as blue and yellow so that she can see how she created the color green when they mixed together.

VARIATION: Give her red and yellow paints to create orange. Or, give her red and blue to make the color purple.

23. Give your toddler various lengths of masking tape to put on a sheet of paper. Then give him a small sponge that has been dipped in paint. When the paint dries, take off the masking tape and admire the design he has created.

24. Use a squeeze bottle and fill it with paint. Give your child this bottle and a piece of paper. Show her how to squeeze the paint out of the bottle. Then give her a brush to spread the paint around on the page.

25. Tape a sheet of bubble wrap to the table. Give your child some finger paint to spread on the bubble wrap.

26. Make your own stamp pad by folding a few squares of paper towels together and moisten them. Place the towels in a tray

such as a Styrofoam tray and pour paint on the towels. Use your stamps.

27. Stick any materials on your child's rolling pin to create interesting prints. For example, add bandages, bunion and corn pads, bubble wrap, or wind yarn around the rolling pin. Then roll her rolling pin in some paint that you have poured into a shallow container. Now roll onto paper.

28. For a different texture in play dough, mix together 4 cups of flour and 1/2 cup of baby oil or vegetable oil. Add some vanilla to the mixture and enjoy its fragrance.

29. Trace various basic shapes such as circles and squares or trace some cookie cutters onto craft foam sheets. Or you could cut out templates to make a scene: the sun, clouds, grass, trees and a house. Then show your toddler how to paint each piece with water and stick them on a patio door or window.

30. Give your toddlers some sheets of tissue paper to tear into pieces. Then show him how to scrunch some of her cut sheets of tissue paper. Spread some glue with a brush onto a sheet of construction paper. Stick all of the tissue pieces onto the page. When he is finished, brush more glue on top.

31. Give her a small booklet of post-it notes and let her put those on a sheet of construction paper. For added enjoyment, give her different sizes of post-it notes and perhaps add additional dot stickers. These post-it notes could be taken off later and used again for this activity.

32. Give your toddler some bandages to put on a sheet of construction paper or even on a colorful paper plate. You could also add cotton balls, gauze pads and cotton swabs.

33. Cut some small rectangles from
    construction paper that can be folded in
    half. Give your child some glue to paste
    half of the rectangle onto a sheet of paper.
    Then have him put a picture inside the
    fold. He can have fun lifting up each flap
    to see what is underneath.

34. Brush some glue on a sheet of paper and
    then give her some sprinkles that can be
    purchased in shaker bottles that are used
    to decorate cookies. Let her shake these
    sprinkles onto the page. Just shake off the
    loose sprinkles from the page when it is all
    dried.

35. Brush some glue on a sheet of paper and
    give her a selection of gift wrapping
    materials such as ribbons, bows and
    wrapping paper to glue onto the paper.

36. Cut up some straws into various lengths.
    Then cut some strips of tape and put it
    along a plastic container for him to pull

off. Show him how to use the tape to secure these straw lengths on a sheet of construction paper.

37. Cut some grocery pictures from some flyers. Give her these pictures to glue onto a paper plate.

38. Give him a sheet of coarse sandpaper and then glue on soft items such as feathers, cotton balls, and small pompoms on the paper.

39. Give your child some pasta such as penne, egg noodles, bow ties and rigatoni to glue onto a paper plate or card stock.

40. Give your toddler some foil strips to tear, crumple and squeeze. Dip the foil into a dish of glue and then glue onto a sheet of construction paper.

41. Give your child a sheet of paper towel to color with her crayons or markers. Then

give her a small spray bottle with water and show her how to spray water on the paper towel. Crumple the towel and then straighten the towel to show her how the colors have blended together.

42. Give your child some muffin liners and show him how to flatten them. Then glue them onto a sheet of construction paper. You could also add some stickers or small pompoms.

43. Give your toddler a shallow pan of paint and a potato masher. Dip the masher into the paint and then press on a sheet of paper.

44. Combine the following ingredients together to make a textured finger paint: 1 cup flour, 2 tablespoons liquid soap, 2/3 cup water and food coloring. Let your child enjoy spreading this on a sheet of paper. Then give her a craft stick to drag across her page.

45. Combine together 1/2 cup cornmeal, 1/2 cup liquid paint and 1/2 cup of liquid glue. Give him a sheet of paper to spread with her fingers. Rather than using paper, you could give him a sheet of aluminum foil for a different texture.

46. Give her a small dish of paint and a pot scrubber. Dip it in the paint and then press it onto the paper.

47. Pour several different colors of paint on a sheet of construction paper. Then place another sheet of construction paper on top of this. Give him a rolling pin to spread the colors over the paper.

48. Place a dollop of finger paint in the center of some paper. Then give her a rubber spatula to spread it around.

49. Give him a plastic drinking cup or more, if you have different sizes. Then show him how to dip each cup into shallow

containers of paint and then press the rim of the cup on a sheet of construction paper.

50. Clip some pompoms to clothespins. Place each pompom near its paint color. Show her how to dip the pompoms into the paint and press onto a sheet of construction paper.

51. Create a collage using cotton balls, tissue paper and any other items. Show your toddler how to crumple small pieces of tissue paper and attach to self-adhesive paper (contact paper). You can make seasonal collages by adding appropriate items. For autumn, you can add colored leaves and pinecones that you have collected from a walk with your toddler.

CHAPTER 4:

SENSORY ACTIVITIES

Sensory play is an important part of a child's development as he learns to interpret and engage with his environment.

Many parents do not enjoy sensory activities since it creates too much mess! However, the mess is manageable if you have a drop cloth under the table where your child or children are working. Consider where you will do these activities as some may be done outside or in the bathtub.

If your child does not like getting his fingers messy, give him a variety of brushes to use or let him wear thin mittens. Remember that each one of these activities should provide enjoyment not frustration and anxiety.

IMPORTANT: Close Adult Supervision is Required with Each of These Activities

1. Chill several Tablespoons of body lotion in the fridge. Then place a large spoonful of "warm" lotion on a cookie sheet. Encourage your toddler to smell the lotion and then use the lotion as finger paint. Then give him some of the cold lotion to play with. Talk to him about the different temperatures.

2. In a large bowl, add water in small amounts to a white soap powder such as Ivory Snow until you have a thin dough. Place 2 - 3 tablespoons of this mixture on a cookie sheet for finger painting.

3. Use one box of cornstarch and add water and food coloring to your mixture. This can be used as finger paint or you can spread it out on a cookie sheet and have

her run a small car through it. Refrigerate the dough in a plastic bag or container for another day of play.

4. Prepare a package of pudding and pour some of it onto a cookie sheet. Let her enjoy finger painting and licking her fingers through out this process.

5. Pour a large bag of black beans into a long, shallow plastic container. Then add a couple of car tracks from Fast Track or Hot Wheel sets or just cut out a track from some cardboard. Include pedestrians that you have from your child's toys and some building blocks.

VARIATION: You could also include any small villages that you might have in your Christmas decorations. Cut out the ends of a small shoe box or photo box to make a tunnel for the car to drive through. Add a few large rocks and any road signs that you might have from any other toy sets. Give him a squirt bottle and a cloth to wash his cars. There may also be room to add a small upright box as the gas station. Inside the box, add an eye dropper filled with water for the gas. Give her a variety of spoons to play with the black beans.

6. Prepare 2 or 3 colors of gelatin ahead of time. When set, place globs of each color on a cookie sheet and use for finger painting!

7. Pour some bubble bath into the bathtub and let your child enjoy playing in the bath tub. You could also blow bubbles for her to pop.

8. Give her two bowls - one filled with water and another one empty. Place a sponge in the bowl of water and show her how to squeeze the sponge over the empty bowl to fill it with water.

9. Place 3 rocks and 3 pompoms in a basket. As she holds each one of them, bring to her attention how the rock is hard and the pompom is soft. See if she can sort them into two different piles.

10. Give her some yogurt and some graham wafers and show her how to "finger paint" the yogurt on these items. She will enjoy eating her finger painting project!

11. Fill a large plastic container with snow. Give your child sand molds, a shovel and a pail. Also, give your child a small container of items that could be used to accessorize the small snowman that you could help him make. After the two of you are finished playing with the snow, give your child a squirt bottle filled with water to see what happens to the snowman when you squirt him with water.

VARIATION: If you don't have snow, fill the container with white cotton balls. You could also make a snowman with round Styrofoam balls.

12. Fill a small jar almost to the top with water. Take turns putting a penny into the container. See whose penny causes the water to overflow.

13. On a regular basis, put different items in a large plastic jar with a screw on lid. She will enjoy opening the jars and playing with the items. These items can be small toys, household items, mittens or scarves etc.

14. Give her some play dough and after she has given the lump some sort of shape, give her a straw or a craft stick to poke holes in it.

15. Boil some eggs and take off the shells. Let your child play with the shells. Give her a

child's plastic hammer or child's rolling pin to crush them. You may want to give her mittens to wear since the eggs shells can be a little sharp.

16. Put in a sealable plastic bag a small amount of two colors of paint. Place that bag inside another bag and seal. Let your toddler squish and knead the bag and discover what new color of paint she is creating.

17. Use expanding aqua gel beads and test the texture after you soak them in water for 6 hours. Put them in a rectangular plastic container for him to enjoy putting his hands through the soft, "squishy" beads. Give him measuring cups, scoops and spoons to enjoy playing with these beads.

18. Make the following Salt Play Dough Recipe and give your toddler a small rolling pin and cookie cutters. Mix the following together: 1 cup salt, 1 cup flour

and 1/2 cup of warm water.

19. Open a tin of Biscuit Mix or thaw some frozen bread dough and let him create shapes with the dough. Place these shapes on a greased cookie sheet. She could also sprinkle a mixture of sugar and cinnamon on top of her shapes. Bake and enjoy.

20. Cut a sheet of coarse sandpaper into 6 pieces. Do the same with a smooth sheet of paper. Place one of the coarse sheets and one of the smooth sheets on the table. Use your fingertips to touch them and comment, "This one feels rough". "This one feels smooth". Give her one of the other pieces. "Is it smooth? Is it rough? Let's put it on top of the other one that is rough." Continue doing this with all of the pieces. Put the two piles in random order and begin sorting again.

VARIATION: Add a square piece of sandpaper that isn't as coarse or as smooth as the two you have already used. You could begin mentioning how one is "a little bit coarse" and the other one is "very coarse" or rough to the touch.

21. Pour into a shallow plastic container a large bag of bird seed. Add any farm animals, a small tractor and truck from your child's toys. Include a small box of black beans or popcorn so that your child can feed the animals. Give your child a large spoon and ladle to play with the bird feed and popcorn.

22. Use some sort of drawstring bag such as a shoe bag for this activity. Give your child three different items that he is familiar with. Name each one of them. It can be a piece of fruit, some Duplo and a toy car. Then put a tea towel over the items and quietly slip one of them into the bag. Let him feel the outside of the bag and then let him put his hand into the bag and feel the

item. Can he guess what it is?

VARIATION: Put all three items in the bag and see if she can find the item you ask her for, merely through touch.

23. Play with some "sandy play dough": Put into a saucepan 2 cups of playable sand, 1 cup cornstarch and 1 1/2 cups of water. Cook over low heat stirring the mixture until it thickens. Remove the dough from the pan and knead it when it is cool enough to handle.

24. Collect a selection of different fabrics such as muslin, felt, cotton, satin, silk, and velvet. Have several of each piece of fabric so that you can have her sort them after she has felt them.

25. Create putty from the following recipe: Mix 1 part liquid starch and 2 parts white glue. Experiment with the amounts until it reaches the consistency of putty. The more

glue that is added, the more flexible the material. If you put too much liquid starch, the putty will become too brittle. If you refrigerate this putty in an airtight container, it will last 2 to three days.

26. Place several small toys into a plastic container or a bundt cake pan or a gelatin mold, and then fill 3/4 full of water. Freeze over night. Take the ice out of the container and then place on a tray. Give your child a spoon and this sculpture to play with. Talk about how the ice is gradually melting and turning back into water. As it begins to melt, she can use her spoon to gradually retrieve the small toys.

27. Make some Kool-Aid Dough and give your child some cookie cutters to play with the dough. Mix together 1 cup of flour with 1 cup of boiling water. Add 3 tablespoons of corn oil, 1/2 cup salt and 1 package of Kool-Aid.

28. Spread some baking soda on a tray and then pour drops of vinegar on various parts of the tray. Your child will enjoy watching the chemical reaction when baking soda and vinegar are mixed together. Then give her a spoon, foil plate and an eyedropper to play with the mixture.

29. Give your child various spices to smell and give her the names of them. Let her smell the same ones every day for a week and see if she can eventually identify them. Then introduce her to a new set of spices to smell.

30. Create an ice skating rink by freezing water in a long shallow plastic container. Then give your child toys such as her Little People to "skate" on the ice. Your child may want to wear mitts to keep his hands warm when he is engaged in this activity.

31. Pour into a long shallow plastic container some bird feed. Include such items as a round plastic container filled with glass rocks for water, toy dinosaurs, small rocks, plastic eggs, container of popcorn, and plastic vegetation. For added fun, give her a magnifying glass to look more closely at the items in the bin. Remember to give her an assortment of containers and spoons for interacting with this sensory bin. Children especially enjoy using funnels.

32. Fill a container with squares of different kinds of fabrics such as wool, minky, fake fur, silk, satin, sateen, cotton, jersey etc. Prepare matching squares for each fabric. Then see if your child can sort them. When she becomes quite familiar with the fabrics, see if she can find the matches when her eyes are closed or blindfolded.

33. Purchase some herbs to show her what they look like and of course let her enjoy smelling them. You could also decide to grow some herbs together in a pot in your

kitchen or if it is summer, in a pot outside.
Teach her how to water them and to
watch them grow. When they begin to
grow, show her how to crush the herbs
with a small mortar and pestle and use
them in your cooking. Or perhaps make a
small bowl of potpourri to enjoy the
fragrance.

34. Set a large plastic container filled with
    water into the bathtub. Your child will get
    wet so you may decide to put on only her
    diaper or her bathing suit. Then set your
    child in the bathtub giving her an
    assortment of bath toys to use such as
    cups, bowls, funnels, empty squeeze
    bottles, sponges or any of her regular bath
    toys.

35. Pour into a long, shallow plastic container
    a large container of Fruit Loop Cereal.
    Then add all sorts of birthday items such
    as: candles, party hats, muffin liners,
    disposable "Happy Birthday" plates and
    cups, small party bags, etc. Your child can

have fun with this bin any time of the year but it also may be a great way to get her excited about her own birthday party approaching.

36. Place some parchment paper on a cookie sheet. Then pour some sand on top. Show your child how to "write" in the sand using her finger, a craft stick, and a straw.

37. Tape two cardboard rolls of empty toilet paper together to make binoculars. Walk around the house or outside looking through them. What does she see? If you own a child's binoculars, use these as you explore and discover how things look different through them.

38. Place some small items in a bowl or container. Then pour over these items some rice or bird seed. Now give your child some spoons to find the hidden items.

39. To focus on taste, put a small piece of lemon in a dish and a spoonful of honey in another dish. When she tastes each one, tell her that the lemon is sour and the honey is sweet. You could also give her a taste of salt and then give her some potato chips or popcorn explaining that these taste good since they are salty.

40. Hide some items around the room for your child to find. Talk about how she found them by being able to see so well.

CHAPTER 5:

BOOKS
TO READ

The picture books in this chapter have been chosen to help your toddler develop her ability to "pretend play" and to better understand and enjoy the world around her.

Choose books in any order according to what is available at your local library. Be sure to reserve several books each time since you can usually keep them for three weeks.

Your own interest and enthusiasm will largely determine the extent of your toddler's response to the book. Therefore, read each book with great expression by changing the tone and volume of your voice. Keep her engaged by pointing out different things on the page and asking her to point to them.

Develop her curiosity and anticipation as you show her the cover of the book and ask, "I wonder what this story will be about?" Read the first page of the story and speculate who will be on the next page or what will be happening.

You may think that some of these activities are time consuming as you show her how to pretend play. However, you will be pleasantly surprised how she will begin repeating these pretend play activities on her own when you are busy doing something else.

IMPORTANT: Close Adult Supervision is Required with Each Of These Activities.

1. Who Sank The Boat? by Pamela Allen

If you have a large cardboard box, use it for a boat. Otherwise, place a small blanket on the floor and tell your toddler, "Let's pretend this blanket is our boat." Ask her to collect all of her plush animals and dolls to go for a boat ride. As she gets them organized on the boat, remind her that if too many animals get on the boat, the boat may tip just like it did in the story. Save the smallest plush animal for last. Finally, when you are all sitting in the boat, reach for the smallest animal and put him in the boat. Grab your toddler's hands and have fun rolling out of the boat.

Another day that you read this book, fill a tub or sink with water and collect items that can float and other items that will sink. Let your toddler play with these items in the water. Here are some suggestions for items: paper clip, cork, plastic boat, penny, sponge, crayon, cotton ball, feather, metal toy car, plastic egg, paper, plastic straw, and a crumpled ball of aluminum foil.

2. THUMP, THUMP, Rat-a-Tat-Tat by Gene Baer

Both you and your child will need a set of drums that can be easily made by wrapping a circle of wax paper around the top of a round container and secured with a strong elastic band. Play some marching music and begin tapping on your drums. Practice certain rhythms such as "thump, thump, thump" and "Rat – a – ta -tat." Encourage your child to copy your rhythms. Also, tap your drums loudly and then softly.

3. <u>Where's My Teddy?</u> by Jez Alborough

Before reading this book, hide your toddler's teddy bear or favorite plush animal somewhere in the house. After reading the story, tell your toddler that he needs to search through the house to find his own teddy. Remember to tell him to pretend that he needs a nap after he finds his teddy. Or perhaps he will actually need a nap!

4. <u>Big Red Barn</u> by Margaret Wise Brown

Build a barn with cardboard boxes and building blocks. Put in the barn any plastic animals or plush animals that you would find on a farm. Give the animals food to eat from your child's play food or give some of the animals real food. For example, give the horses small pieces of carrots and apples that your toddler will also enjoy eating. There were many animals mentioned in this book that your toddler can imitate with the appropriate sounds.

5. Hit The Ball Duck by Jez Alborough

    Give your child an empty wrapping paper tube to use as a bat. Throw her a balloon to hit. Set up some bases in the house for her to run to after she hits the balloon.

    Be sure to show her a real baseball and bat.

6. Which Hat Is That? by Anna G. Hines

    Put into a suitcase or tote bag various kinds of hats such as a baseball cap, a baby's hat, cowboy hat, hockey helmet, sun hat, a child's fireman's hat, a toque, and any other kinds of hats that you have. Let him have fun taking them out of the bag and trying them on. Help him use his imagination. When he puts on a baseball cap, ask him if he is going to a baseball game, or a fireman's hat to help someone, or a toque to build a snowman outside.

7. <u>My Car</u> by Byron Barton

Fill a dishpan with soap and water and have your toddler wash her toy cars.

Create a road with masking tape and suggest he drives the car to get some oil for the car, to go shopping, and to look for a place to park. Remind him to "honk his horn" when some people start crossing the road. In other words, you are showing him how to repeat what occurred in the book.

8. Clap Your Hands by Lorinda Bryan Cauley

Read this book to your child first and then when you read it the second time, have your child do all the motions from clapping her hands, stomping her feet, shaking her arms and "then take a seat."

9. Humpty Dumpty by Salina Yoon

Humpty Dumpty is put back together in this book. Help your toddler build a wall with cardboard boxes or building blocks and place a plastic egg on top. Say the nursery rhyme as you push the egg off the wall! Break open the plastic egg and show her how Humpty is broken. Give her some bandages and tell her that she can put him back together again.

Give him a real egg to examine. Point out the yolk and the egg white to him. Boil an egg and let him examine it also – and then enjoy eating it.

10. <u>Pancakes For Breakfast</u> by Tomie dePaola

After you read this book together, make some pancakes together.

11. <u>Snowballs</u> by Lois Ehlert

Make snowballs and snowmen with real snow if seasonally appropriate or make snowballs with some food. Use a Rice Krispies Square Recipe or a Popcorn Balls Recipe to make food snowmen.

12. <u>Spot Goes To The Park</u> by Eric Hill

Help your toddler create an indoor playground. Use masking tape on the floor as a balance beam. Tape together two empty wrapping paper tubes and set on an incline to roll Ping-Pong balls down. Put some sand or pretend sand such as packing foam chips into a long rectangular container. And give her a small pail and shovel. Of course, if the weather permits, take her to an actual playground.

13. <u>Wrapping Paper Romp</u> by Patricia Hubbell

Put a small toy into a box and wrap. Let your toddler unwrap the box and then remind him how the baby in this story prefers to play with the wrapping paper and the box. Therefore, encourage him to crumple the paper into balls – with your help. Then throw these balls into the empty box.

14. <u>Spot Goes to The Library</u> by Eric Hill

Tell your toddler she is going to set up her books in a room and pretend the room is the library. Choose a spot where she can sign out her books from the library. Suggest that she gets her dolls and animals and set them up in a circle for story time at the library. You, the librarian, could then read a book to them. What book is your toddler going to choose to "sign out" from the library?

After the books are all put away, you may want to go visit the library.

15. <u>Spot Loves Sports</u> by Eric Hill

Set up a goal and kick a ball through the goal and pretend you are playing soccer.

Glue a craft stick onto a firm paper plate to use as a racquet. Then set up some boxes as the net. Use your "racquets" to hit a balloon across your net and pretend you and your child are playing tennis.

Set up a laundry basket and throw a ball into your basket and pretend you are playing basketball.

Have a race from one side of the room to the other.

Pretend you are riding a bicycle as you lie on your backs and raise your legs to bicycle.

Show your child pictures of the following if you do not have the actual balls: a soccer ball, a tennis racquet and ball, and a basketball.

16. <u>Frog, Where Are You?</u> by Mercer Mayer

Put a plush animal inside a bucket to pretend he is your child's pet. Then have your child pretend he is sleeping while you hide the plush animal. Begin an adventure looking for the frog similar to what you just read by crawling under the table, jumping over some pillows, and walking downstairs until you find this plush animal sitting beside some other plush animals. You wave goodbye to the other plush animals as you take the one "back home."

Have your toddler pretend she is the frog and make lots of "ribbit" sounds as she leaps around the room. Add "lily pads" to hop onto by taping some green construction paper on the floor.

17. <u>I Went Walking</u> by Sue Williams

Give your child a laundry basket or a basket with a handle so that he can collect his dolls and animals that you have set throughout the house as he goes for a walk.

18. <u>Boo Hoo, Boo-Boo</u> by Marilyn Singer

Use a child's medical kit or just a wet face cloth, some bandages and gauze as she pretends that her dolls and plush animals have hurt themselves and need her help.

19. <u>We're Going On a Bear Hunt</u> by Michael Rosen

Make a bear's cave by placing a blanket over a chair and then begin your bear hunt. Crawl with your toddler under tables, climb stairs, and walk across pillows until you have reached the bear's cave. When you "see" the bear, run away repeating your route until you run into the bedroom and crawl into bed.

Watch Michael Rosen's video on youtube.com as he narrates this story using hand motions.

20. <u>Pizza At Sally's</u> by Monica Wellington

The author includes a recipe for pizza at the back of the book. Therefore, together make the dough and add toppings to make your own pizza.

If you don't want to make the dough, just purchase a prepared pizza crust. Ask your child to name the toppings that she is adding to the pizza.

21. <u>Spot's Hide and Seek</u> by Eric Hill

Hide some of your child's plush animals before you begin this activity. Tell your child to be like Spot and close his eyes while you count to ten. Then tell him to find all of his plush animal friends who are hiding. You could also take turns hiding from each other. Talk about how each of Spot's friends are found because they are giggling. Giggle together!

22. <u>Sea, Sand, Me</u> by Patricia Hubbell

Create your own beach by putting a blanket on the floor and pretend it is the beach. Lay your beach towels on top of this blanket. Pack a tote bag with beach items such as sun hat, sandals, beach ball, pail and shovel and bathing suit. Let her enjoy taking out these items to play with. Play with the beach ball by rolling it back and forth to each other. Make sure you and your toddler prepare a snack or lunch to take to the beach. Before you read this book, make a big batch of play dough so that you can make play dough castles. Add some seashells and twigs to the "sand castle."

The following recipe for play dough makes a large batch for your sand castle: 2 cups sand, 1 cup cornstarch, 2 teaspoons cream of tartar, 1 1/2 cups boiling water

She may also want to put on her bathing suit and go swimming in the "lake" or bath tub!

23. <u>Cars</u> by Patricia Hubbell

Give your toddler a tour of your car as you point out the following: steering wheel, hubcaps, wheels, headlights, windshield wipers, turning signal, and gas tank. You could even open up the hood and show him inside the engine.

After the tour of your car, set up a board or large cardboard on an incline for your child to drive his cars.

24. Firefighters by Patricia Hubbell

Check out the following website which gives simple instructions to make a fireman's hat. http://www.makingfriends.com/firemans _hat.htm. You will need one sheet of red craft foam and scraps of white and black craft foam. After your child puts on her fireman's hat, give her an empty squirt bottle to put out fires.

Scrunch up some yellow, orange and red tissue paper and set these papers throughout the house as pretend fires. Encourage your toddler to jump inside his pretend fire truck and make the appropriate siren sounds. He can "drive" through the house looking for fires to put out using his bottle.

Drive to your local fire station and look at the large fire truck. Also, why not take some cookies to give the firefighters.

25. Caillou: The Shopping Trip by Nicole Nadeau

This book provides a great opportunity to teach your child how to put on his own coat. Place the coat on the floor and have your child stand behind it facing the collar of the coat. He leans forward and places both of his arms into the sleeves of the coat and then pulls the coat over his head. It will be clearer if you check out the following website for a visual demonstration:

How to Teach Your Kids to Put on a Coat:
http://www.youtube.com/watch?v=iEn CZQeJ6tI

Give your child a basket or a child's cart and begin pretend shopping. Place food from your pantry or from his food play set on low tables and shelves. As she shops, mention how the little boy in the book began playing in the store and lots of onions fell on the floor. You could reenact that scene. If you have a child's cash register, set this up also on a table where she pays for her groceries.

26. <u>Let's Dance, Little Pookie</u> by Sandra Boynton

After reading this book, tell your child that she can pretend to be Pookie and that you will pretend to be Pookie's mother. Play some fast upbeat music while the two of you do some of the actions that the book mentions: hopping up and down, marching and reaching for the sky and reaching for the toes. Then of course you "shimmy, shimmy, shake in our very own style." Finish your dance with a bow.

27. <u>Maisy Goes Camping</u> by Lucy Cousins

Have your child collect her dolls and plush animals to go on a camping trip. Make a tent together with a blanket and props. Have your child put her animals and dolls in the tent. Then share a snack or lunch on the floor in front of your tent. Encourage your child to play an instrument and sing a song like Maisy did in the book. Then sit inside the tent to read a book together. When you say that you are pretending it is nighttime and you must go to sleep in the tent, you will notice that it is too small for everyone to sleep inside. Have your toddler create a bed for her animals outside of the tent.

28. <u>Row, Row, Row Your Boat</u> illustrated by Annie Kubler

This book provides an easy activity as you merely copy what these little babies are doing during the song.

29. <u>Growing Vegetable Soup</u> by Lois Ehlert

If you are reading this book during the spring or summer, you will be able to show your child a real garden - either yours or the neighbors. Regardless, show him how a gardener plants seeds and how the seed gradually grows into a specific vegetable. Give him some seeds to plant either outside or in a pot for inside. Each day, look at the pot and talk about how the plant needs sunshine and water for the plant to grow.

Show her the vegetables mentioned in the book: zucchini, squash, carrots, corn, green beans, tomatoes, broccoli and cabbage. Show her some of these vegetables each day and see if she can identify them when you name them.

Make the vegetable soup recipe that is included at the back of this book or your own favorite vegetable soup recipe.

30. I Stink by Kate and Jim McMullan

This book includes a CD that narrates this story. What makes it interesting is that on Track 1 on the CD, the narration has page-turn signals. You could show your toddler how you know when to turn the page by listening for this signal. See if your toddler will begin to know when to turn the page by himself.

Reading this book gives you an opportunity to show your toddler items in your garbage that will be recycled and other items that will go to a landfill as garbage. Show her your large garbage can and recycling container that you use. If you compost, obviously show her what you do with apple peelings and bananas etc. Show her your container of bottles that must be returned to the bottle depot so that they can be used again. Explain how it is best for us to not have a lot of garbage since the places where they take the garbage are getting too full

Give him a large cardboard box. Make a large hole on one end to tie a rope for her to pull. Tell him that this box is his garbage truck. Now pull it through some rooms for him to collect garbage. Beforehand, set out on the floor various items that he can pretend are to be collected for garbage or recycling. Perhaps, even add a bottle or two that needs to be taken to the bottle depot. When he returns from his garbage collection, have him sort his garbage and place in the appropriate receptacles.

It would be great if your toddler could also have an opportunity to actually see the large truck arrive in front of her own home to collect all of the garbage and the recycling items. The workers would be really appreciative if you and your toddler plan to bake cookies and surprise them with a container of cookies.

31. Clifford Goes to The Doctor by Norman Bridwell

After reading this book, set up a pretend area for your toddler to be a veterinarian. Either use a coffee table or a child-sized table for the examining table. You may have a child's medical kit that includes a stethoscope, a needle and tongue depressor. If you don't, just use an old cosmetic bag or shaving kit to put such items in: a magnifying glass, bandages, long strips of crepe paper streamers to bandage her plush animals and a digital food scale. Suggest that she collects all of her plush animals since they need to come and see the veterinarian for their checkups.

32. Bathtub Blues by Kate McMullan

A CD accompanies this story that allows you to dance after you read the story. Or you could listen to the song while you turn the pages of the book.

Your toddler most likely has his bath just before he goes to bed. Why not surprise him and suggest that he has a bath in the middle of the day. Make it a really fun time including bubble bath. Show him how to make a bubble beard just like the baby Charlotte did. If you have some bubble solution, blow bubbles in front of him in the bath tub and see if he can pop them.

33. Sheep Take A Hike by Nancy Shaw

Give your toddler some items to pack in a small child's backpack and suggest that she goes on a pretend hike. As the two of you travel through the house, climb some stairs as you pretend you are climbing up hill, and of course, walk down the stairs as you pretend you are walking down the hill. Crawl under chairs and tables as you pretend you are squeezing through trees and underbrush. Lead the way so that you can show her what it means to "zig" and "zag". Or before you begin this hike, place some painter's tape or masking tape on the floor in a zigzag pattern to walk on. As you "hike," drop some cheerios on the floor to find your way back "home." On your return home, begin picking up the cheerios that is indicating how you find your way home. During the hike, she can open up her backpack and have the treat she packed.

Go for a short hike outside.

34. <u>The Toolbox</u> by Anne & Harlow Rockwell

This book names a lot of tools that, if you own, you could show him. Of course, many of these tools such as the saw are dangerous so it would be a good time to tell him how he can only look at them with mommy or daddy since he could get hurt.

You will need the following supplies for your toddler: a child's plastic hammer, a child's plastic saw, golf tees, and some Styrofoam. Give these items to her in a basket with a handle or a small toolbox.

Tell him that the golf tees are pretend nails and show him how to use his hammer to hammer the golf tees into his chunk of Styrofoam. Then show him how to use his plastic saw and cut through the Styrofoam.

35. <u>The Little Red Hen</u> by Paul Galdone

Try to get a copy of this book that includes a CD of the author narrating the store. On one track, he narrates the story but has "page-turn signals." Have your child listen for that signal and turn the page.

Talk about how the cat, dog and mouse didn't want to help the red hen. Then ask her if she would like to help you make some bread. Purchase a frozen loaf of bread dough and thaw it the night before. Roll the loaf of bread dough out into a rectangle. Have your child help you spread some butter and cinnamon on this rectangle. Then roll it up, and cut into cinnamon buns. Use floss to cut the rolled dough really easily into buns and place on a cookie sheet. Bake at 350 F for 20 minutes and enjoy eating them!

While the buns are cooking, you could have your child help you make a smoothie. Have her help you put placemats on the table, glasses and plates for the cinnamon buns. Talk about how much fun it is to help each other.

36. <u>If You Give A Moose A Muffin</u> by Laura Numeroff

This moose does a lot of things in this story: he eats muffins, sews on a button, makes sock puppets, makes a mural, and dresses up as a ghost. You could do any of these activities with your toddler. Or you can keep it really simple and together make some muffins!

37. <u>Momma's Magical Purse</u> by Paulette Bogan

Before you read this book, fill up an old purse or small tote bag with many of the items that are described in this book: bandages, sweaters, scarves, food, a small blanket, rain boots, rain coat, umbrella, a small pail, a flyswatter, a rope (skipping rope), facial tissue. Your child will enjoy playing with all of the items in this "magical purse."

38. Airport by Byron Barton

Have your child pretend he is an airplane by holding his arms out and traveling through the room "flying."

Set up some chairs so that you have an aisle in the middle. Tell your toddler that she is the pilot who is going to fly this airplane. Have her get her dolls and plush animals to be the passengers. For extra fun, give your toddler a white shirt and dark tie to wear when she is a pilot. Give her the lid of a large ice cream pail to use as her steering wheel. When she sits in the pilot's seat, ask her if the plane is ready for takeoff. Tell her that you are the flight attendant who takes care of the passengers. While she flies the plane, you can role-play how a flight attendant tells everyone to wear a seat belt. And you can serve people food and drinks. Then switch roles so that your toddler can be a flight attendant. Perhaps replace the tie with a scarf for a change in costume. This time you can pretend that you are a passenger receiving her care.

You could also consider driving your toddler to the airport to watch the airplanes land.

39. <u>Baby Danced the Polka</u> by Karen Beaumont

Gather all of your toddler's dolls and plush animals and encourage him to dance with each one of them. Enjoy dancing to a fast polka!

40. <u>Max Cleans Up</u> by Rosemary Wells

After you read this book together, give your toddler lots of opportunities to help you sort socks, fold towels, and clean various rooms!

41. Left Hand Right Hand by Janet Allison Brown

   Do any of the activities in the book to help your toddler understand how she has a left hand and a right hand.

42. Mrs. McNosh Hangs Up Her Wash By Sarah Weeks

   Hang up a rope or skipping rope attached between two chairs. Give your toddler lots of clothes pegs. Give her a basket of items that were mentioned in this book to hang: dresses, shirts, underwear, nightgowns, skirts, stockings, shoes, paper, dog (plush animal), a hat, etc.

43. Rock – a – Baby Band by Kate McMullan

   A CD comes with this book and after you collect various "instruments", play the CD and dance as you drum with your pot and wooden spoon, or shake a tambourine.

44. <u>Baby Day</u> by Susan Heyboer O'Keefe

Play the same games with your own toddler as mentioned in the book: throw him up in the air, chase him around the room, play with a ball, play peek-a-boo, play whirly-go, play pat-a-cake, blow bubbles, and play "piggy count". Then give your toddler his doll and tell him to take care of him by playing with him, feeding him, changing him, taking him for a walk, rocking him and putting him to bed.

45. <u>Maisy goes to The Hospital</u> by Lucy Cousin

Set up a hospital in a room. Create several beds and place your child's dolls and animals in them as patients. Tell your toddler she is the doctor who needs to take care of all of these patients. Give your toddler some gauze to wrap one of the doll's legs to pretend this doll hurt her leg on a trampoline. If you have a medical kit, encourage her to use her needle, her stethoscope and bandages. Show her how to make up a conversation between the patients and the doctor.

46. <u>One Rainy Day</u> by M. Christina Butler

Put into a suitcase or tote bag clothes that you would wear on a hot sunny day and clothes that you would need to wear to walk outside on a rainy day. Let your child take these items out of the suitcase and sort them into two piles: sunny day clothing and rainy day clothing.

Then tell him that he is going to pretend that it is a rainy day and to put on his rain gear. Go on youtube.com and play some rain music and let her walk through the house carrying a child's size umbrella. Beforehand, tape black construction paper on the floor and tell him that he can jump into these mud puddles.

Whenever you have a rainy day, go for a walk outside.

47. <u>The Snowy Day</u> by Ezra Jack Keats

Have an indoor snowy day. Place some bubble wrap on the floor and let her walk on it as she pretends that her feet are crunching in the snow. Show her how to walk with her toes pointing out and then pointing in.

Take some white socks and tie each one to make snowballs and begin throwing snowballs at each other. Then see how many snow balls he can throw into a basket.

Show her how to lie on the floor and make angels.

Create a hill with pillows and then place a blanket across it. Let him climb the mountain of snow.

48. We're Going On A Picnic by Pat Hutchins

If it is a nice day outside, make a lunch and go for a real picnic. However, you can also have fun planning your picnic inside. Have your toddler help you cut up some strawberries, apples and pears, and make some sandwiches for your picnic. Show her how to cut a banana using a plastic knife. Then have her help you pack plates, napkins, glasses, juice and the lunch into a container. Remember to pack a book to read together and perhaps a ball to play with. Then decide where you want to lay your blanket for your picnic.

You may decide to dress for the picnic so that even if it is a cold wintery day, turn up the heat and put on your shorts and sunglasses! Have your toddler pack some play food for her dolls on this picnic also.

CHAPTER 6:

LANGUAGE DEVELOPMENT

Gayle Jervis & Kristen Jervis Cacka

No activity can replace the importance of the conversations you have with your child. However, the following activities are helpful conversation starters while at the same time, they will increase your child's awareness and understanding of various words and various language concepts.

One tool we will be using in this section is a Mystery Box. Choose a box that has a separate lid. To create added interest for your child, wrap the bottom of the box and lid separately in fun paper. You could change the paper seasonally.

IMPORTANT: Close Adult Supervision is Required with Each of These Activities.

1. In a suitcase, include various shirts, some small and some large. Also, include sweaters, some small and some large. Can she identify a shirt and a sweater? See if she can sort them by type and then by size. She may want to try on some of the shirts and sweaters.

2. In your mystery box, choose items from the kitchen to put into this box: wooden spoon, plastic container, funnel and some measuring cups. Tell him the names and then see if he can pick up the correct one when you name the item. Give him a large bowl of pompoms or rice and let him enjoy using these items.

3. You will need a turntable that if you don't already have can be found in any store that sells kitchenware. Collect several photos of family or friends for your turntable. Have

her spin the turntable and whatever photo stops in front of her, explain who this person is. Is it a photo of an aunt, uncle, grandma, grandpa, mom or dad? This is a great way for her to learn names of family who she does not get the opportunity to see that often.

4. To teach the words "push" and "pull", tie a string on one of his cars. Then place some masking tape on the hallway floor. Place the car on this tape and then tell him to push his car down the hallway. After he does that, tell him to take the string and pull the car back to the start.

5. Take photos of your child throughout one day recording her getting dressed, having breakfast, brushing her teeth, playing, doing some of these activities, eating lunch, going for a nap, having an afternoon snack, playing with toys, eating supper, taking a bath and finally putting on her pajamas. Put these photos in an album and discuss them with her. You could even

give her just a few of the photos to see if she can put them in the right order.

6. Create a "Who Is It?" book by purchasing a small spiral notebook. Glue a photo or a magazine picture on the right side of each page. Then cut the page on the left hand side into several wide horizontal strips cutting within a couple of inches of the spiral. Your toddler can cover the picture on the right with the strips. Then turn over one strip at a time, gradually revealing more of the picture. Ask your child to guess what the picture is.

7. Collect pictures of people who show various emotions: Find someone who is laughing, smiling, crying, angry and sad. As you look at the pictures, try to imitate the look and say the word it describes. Talk about how it is okay to have these feelings. Don't show all of these photos at once until you have slowly introduced them to him over a period of time.

8. Learn the vocabulary words "big" and "small". Give your child a large ball such as a beach ball. Roll the ball back and forth to one another and talk about how big the ball is. Then give her a small ball such as a ping pong ball and roll the ball and talk about how small the ball is. Now, see if she can distinguish the two balls by asking her to roll the big ball to you.

9. Discuss the words "big and small". Mention how you are big and he is small. Give him some adult clothes to put on and laugh together as you tell him they are too big on him. Then you try to put on some of his clothes and tell him how they are too small for you to wear.

10. Another activity to explore "big and small" is by giving your child a container or jar with a number of items to put into the jar. Give her items that will fit into the jar and others that are too big.

11. In your mystery box, collect items that will help him understand the word "short." Include different lengths of pencils, string, straws, toy cars and books. Take two items out of the box and ask, "which one is short." Lay the two items on the table so that he can see which one is longer. Keep doing this with your various items.

12. To understand the word "short," gather your child's dolls and plush animals to see which one of them is the shortest. Then measure your child's height leaving a pencil mark on a wall. Then you stand and mark your height. Explain how your child is short and you are tall.

13. Discuss the word "long" by taking a long string or measuring tape and pulling it out as far as it can go in your room. Talk about how long that string or tape is. Lay a short string beside the long string to see the difference.

14. Gather various sizes of shoes, and together place them on a long line of masking tape, Talk about which shoe is long and which shoe is short. Then sit on the floor across from each other putting your foot against your child's foot. Ask, which foot is long?

15. Discuss the word "long" by giving her a few strands of spaghetti, and talk about how they are long. Then break one in half and put it under the long piece of spaghetti and mention how that one is short. You could even give her a hot dog bun and a small bun and mention how the first bun is long.

16. Show pictures of people with various lengths of hair as you talk about long and short.

17. Give your child some blocks or empty boxes to stack in order to discuss the word "tall." Go for a walk outside and point out trees and buildings that are tall.

18. In your mystery box, place items that are rough. You will need a sheet of sandpaper and glue to make a collage of these rough items. In your box you could include a pinecone, a bottle cap, toothpick, bark, a small piece of carpet, and a textured, rough piece of wallpaper. As you pull out each item, have your child hold it and feel it as you discuss how it feels rough. Then put some glue on the sheet of sandpaper and have him glue the item onto the sandpaper. Continue doing this with each item. Then give him a magnifying glass to look more closely at each of these rough items. When the collage is fully dried, have him run his hand over each item and again mention how rough it feels.

19. Talk about the word "rough" by mixing some sand into some finger paint and as she finger paints, again talk about how rough the paint feels. Or, you could add some salt or sand to her play dough.

20. In a suitcase, add items that are smooth. For example, you could add a silk scarf, a cotton t-shirt, a hard covered book, a smooth rock, a leaf, and a ping pong ball. In your talk about what is smooth, ask him to feel his smooth face and then to feel your smooth face. Take a bottle of body lotion out of the suitcase to put on his legs and your legs and talk about how the cream makes your legs, feel so smooth.

21. Talk about the word "soft" by putting some soft items into your mystery box. Include a feather, a facial tissue, cotton balls, pompoms, velvet, and a soft plush animal. After she has felt all of these items, ask her to throw each one into a laundry basket or bucket. Ask her if these items made any sound. No? That's because they are so soft and light.

22. In your mystery box, add items that are hard such as Duplo blocks, a small board, a wooden spoon, a button, a rock, a clothes peg, a penny, and a mug. Let your

child handle each item and tell him that
these items are NOT soft but they are
hard. Give him some pennies to drop into
a pail. Have him notice that dropping the
pennies into a pail makes a sound. Why?
Because the item is hard. Have him drop
some cotton balls into the pail to remind
him that soft items do not make a noise.

23. Create a mystery box of opposites.
    Combine the items that are soft and hard
    such as a cotton ball and a rock. As she
    takes each item out of the box, see if she
    can tell you which item is soft and which
    item is hard.

    VARIATION: Use rough and smooth
    objects in your mystery box. As she takes
    each item out of the box, see if she can tell
    you what items are rough and what items
    are smooth.

24. See how well your toddler understands the
    words "inside" and "outside". Place a rope

on the floor in the shape of a circle large enough for you and him to sit inside the circle. Read a book sitting inside the circle. Of course, mention that you are inside the circle. Then step out of the circle and explain how you are outside of the circle. Give him some items to line up inside the circle. Then ask him to line up these items outside the circle.

25. To reinforce your toddler's understanding of "inside and outside", place a laundry basket or box on the floor. Then give her some balls or beanbags and tell her to throw them into the box. Look inside the box and say, "The balls are inside the box. Let's find the balls that are outside the box." Do this activity several times.

26. Put in your mystery box, items that will easily demonstrate what it means to have a front and a back. Put in the box a teddy bear, a doll, and a book. Show the front and back of each item. Take your child to a mirror and show him the front of his

body, and then angle the mirror so that he can see his back. Can he show you your front and back? Take him for a walk to the front of your house and then to the back.

27. Show her what it means to walk forward and then backward. Play with her toy cars and trucks. Can she make them go forward? Can she make them go backward? Create an inclined plank leaning against a kitchen chair or sofa. Roll the cars down forward and then backwards. See how far she can walk backwards! Have her put her clothes on backwards!

28. Does your toddler understand what it means to go "over" something? Put a candle on the floor and enjoy saying the traditional verse as you jump over the unlit candle:

> Jack be nimble,
> Jack be quick,
> Jack jump over the candlestick.

29. Pile some pillows on the floor and as he crawls over them, say,

> Red rover,
> Red rover,
> Come on over.

30. Help your child understand the words "over" and "under" by building a bridge with Duplo or some other blocks or even boxes and then have your child drive her toy cars over the bridge. Put some blue construction paper under your bridge to explain that there is water and a bridge is needed for the cars to get across the water.

31. Does your child understand what it means to go "under" something? Without your toddler seeing what you are doing, put some large stickers under some chairs, and then ask her to look under the chair to find them.

32. Play a game of "What is missing?" Put several items on a tray and then put a towel over them. Tell him that there are

three toys under the towel. Then remove one of the toys and ask him what is under the towel? Is something missing?

33. Put a sheet over a table and place some pillows under the table. Have him choose some books to read as he sits under the table. Lay on the floor or even better outside on the grass. Ask him what is above him? And what is under him?

34. In a small suitcase, include various items of clothing that she can learn to identify and perhaps name: scarf, shirt, pants, socks, shoes, and coat.

35. Introduce him to the word "round" by putting inside a tote bag all sizes of balls: beach ball, baseball, ping pong ball, and basketball. Roll these balls back and forth to each other explaining that they roll so well since they are round.

36. To discuss the word "round", make some cookies that can be rolled into balls. A good way to show her how to roll balls is to just place a small piece of dough on the table and then with her palm, roll it around. Or you could just give her some play dough and roll the dough into balls - perhaps you could make a snowman.

37. In your mystery box, gradually pull out circular items such as a plate, a button, a ring, some lids, and a cookie! See if he can show you small circles and large circles. Show him some items like a box or scarf and ask him if these items are circles.

38. Put inside a suitcase clothing that is worn on a hot day and clothing that is worn on a cold day. Talk about them and then see if she can sort them according to whether you would wear this item on a hot day or a cold day.

39. Help your toddler to understand the following concepts: moving close together and moving further apart. Take two plush animals and move them close together and then far apart. Ask him to move them close together again. Then have him move them far apart.

40. In your mystery box, place items that are blue including a blue balloon, a blue marker, blue stickers, and a blue ribbon. Blow up the balloon and attach a blue ribbon or streamers to it. Your child will enjoy marking the balloon with the blue markers and adding stickers to it. Then she can play with the balloon.

41. Play "I Spy" in one of your rooms. For example, "I spy a lamp." Have him run to the lamp and point.

42. Inside a mystery box, put various kinds of fruit. Let her touch them and enjoy their shapes. Cut in half the fruit so that she can

see which ones have seeds or stones. For an older toddler, give her a plastic knife so that she can slice the banana. After you cut up the fruit, she can enjoy a snack.

43. Cut out pictures of transportation vehicles such as a car, truck, motor cycle, and bus. Tape them on a turntable. He spins the turntable and whichever picture stops in front of him, he can try to name.

44. Put bathroom items into the mystery box: comb, brush, toothbrush, toothpaste (with lid screwed on very tightly), soap, shampoo, cream, and cup. Try naming and explaining each item's use.

45. In the mystery box, include items that are red: ribbon, toy, material, wrapping paper, button, food.

46. Place on the table two plastic containers, one of them that has a red pompom and the other has a green pom pom. Then give

her some red and green pompoms to sort into these two containers. Make sure you tell her the name for the new color you are introducing.

47. Cut out pictures of animals and tape on the turntable for him to identify and to give its sound.

48. Put inside your mystery box three books of three different sizes. Then ask her which one is the biggest. Then have her open a small suitcase that contains three toys of different sizes. Which one is the biggest? Which one is the smallest?

49. Have your child imitate you as you reinforce the meaning of the word "small." For example, take small steps, sit on a small chair, take small hops and roll a small ball."

50. Have your toddler better understand the words, "taller" and "smaller" by building two towers of different heights.

51. Put inside your mystery box any items that are green: Duplo, toy car, pom pom, shirt, crayon, green paper, etc. Give her something to wear that is green and declare that it is "Green Day". Take a bag or basket as you walk around the house searching for more items that are green and put some of those items into the bag. After your "search," let your child enjoy playing with his green items.

52. Help your toddler understand the words, "Open" and "Close": Ask your toddler to open her eyes and then close them. Open her mouth and then close her mouth. Open her hands and then close them. Go around the room and find things to open and close such as doors and drawers and cupboards. Give her a container with a lid to open and close, books to open and close, and a purse to open and close.

53. Put inside a suitcase, clothing that is either red, blue or green. Choose items that he may want to try on such as a red fireman's hat, a green baseball hat, and a blue scarf. See if he can sort these items by color.

54. Does your toddler know the names of the rooms in your house? In a suitcase, pack items that belong from different rooms. Ask her to take the item and put it in the correct room.

ACTIVITY SUPPLY LIST

The following supply list contains most of the items that you will need in order to do the activities in this book. Some activities will require additional items that you may already have in your household. However, you may need to buy some items at such stores as Dollar Store and Michaels.

For a printable Activity Supply List, go to our website at busytoddlerhappymom.com. The printable list also includes blanks lines to include your own extra items.

HOUSEHOLD ITEMS

Hats

Gauze, Bandages, Tape, Face Cloth

Tweezers

Cotton Balls

Shoelace

Golf Tees

Clothes Pegs - Wooden & Plastic

Liquid Starch

Exercise Ball

Shower Curtain Ring or Binder Ring

Paint Stir Stick

Masking Tape

Meter Stick or Dowel

Rubber Bands &/Or Ponytail holders

Various types of Sandpaper: Coarse, Medium
    & Fine

Eye Dropper

White Soap Powder such as Ivory Snow

Child-sized Mop or Shortened Mop

Wrapping Paper

Powdered Laundry Soap

Post It Notes - Various Sizes

Small Spiral Notebook

Small Suitcase

Bubble Bath

Body Lotion

Blankets

Stuffed Animals

KITCHEN ITEMS

Wax Paper

Foil

Muffin Tin

Muffin Liners

Sponge

Turntable

Potato Masher

Pot Scrubber

Plastic Cookie Cutters

Colander with Large Holes

Disposable Cups

Firm Paper Plates

Plastic Knives

Turkey Baster

Dried Beans – Various Types

Dried Oats

Foil Pan

Coffee Filters

Paper Towels

Food Coloring

Pudding Package

Jello Powder

Large Box of Salt

Kool-Aid Powder

Pasta – Various Types

Plastic Tablecloth

TOYS

Child's Plastic Saw

Plastic Hammer

Child's Rolling Pin

Child's Umbrella

ITEMS TO SAVE

Empty Wrapping Paper Tube

Empty Paper Towel Tubes

Old Salad Spinner

Empty Baby Wipes Container or Shoe Box

Empty Roll-On Deodorant or Shoe Polish
Bottle

Empty Plastic Pop Bottles

Empty Facial Tissue Boxes

Thin Styrofoam

Small Squeeze Bottle

Bubble Wrap

Old Salt Shaker

CRAFT

Stickers - Various, Round, Square, Hearts,
Animals

Pompom balls

Construction Paper

Pipe Cleaners

Crayons

Velcro Dots

Clear Contact Paper

Flannel

Flannel Board or make your own by wrapping
flannel tightly around a firm piece of
cardboard.

Craft Foam - Red, White, Blue & other
Colors

Tissue Paper - Yellow, Orange, Red & other
Colors

Child's Scissors

Jingle Bells

Narrow Elastic or Ribbon

Chalk

Printer Paper

Ribbon - Various

Non Toxic Liquid Paint in Primary Colors

Non Toxic Powdered Paint in Primary
Colors

Finger Paints - Primary Colors

Finger paint Paper or Freezer Paper

Paint Brushes - Various Types

Small Paint Roller

Paint with Water Books

Fabric - Various Types

White Glue

Tape - Various Types and Colors: Clear Tape, Masking Tape, Painter's Tape

Permanent Black Marker

Craft Sticks

Markers - Non Toxic & Washable

Aqua Gel Beads

Play Dough

Feathers

CONTAINERS

Cardboard Box

Bucket or large Ice Cream Pail

Small Plant Pot

Tote Bag

Long Shallow Plastic Container

Large Plastic Jar with Screw-On Lid

Drawstring Bag

Small Spray Bottle

Laundry Basket

Small Suitcase

MISCELLANEOUS

Beach Ball

Seeds

Ping Pong Ball or other Small Ball

Magnets

Paint Chips

Magnifying Glass

String

Bean bag or Sock filled with Beans

Balloon

Plastic Eggs

Jump Rope

Suction Cups

Bubbles

Rocks

Old Shirt or Plastic Apron

Sand - make sure it is lead free

ADDITIONAL
RESOURCES

The following list of resources is great for supplementing your toddler's activities.

Check out the printable Additional Resources List at busytoddlerhappymom.com. This printable list includes links so you are able to see examples of these products.

Some of the more specialized items such as fun brushes to use for painting can be found at educational stores such as Education Station.

Reusable Melissa and Doug Stickers

Pegboard and Pegs

Wooden Puzzles

Shape Sorter

Child's Tunnel

Stamps & Stamp Pads

Play Food

Child's Medical Kit

Toy Cash Register

Flannel Board (or just purchase some flannel and attach to a firm piece of cardboard)

Wilton's Cookie Cutters

Clean Sand (found at educational stores)

Easel with a chalkboard and a whiteboard:

> Your toddler can enjoy drawing with washable markers and chalk, or add magnets to the whiteboard on these boards. Or you can attach a sheet of paper to the board for him to paint or color.

Mailbox:

> Each day your child will be quite excited to check her mailbox to see what is in it. You can put any of the following items in it: postcards, cards, junk mail, special notes, library book, photos, notes from relatives, a small toy, fun paper for her to write on, and a coloring page.

BOOKS

Books for Babies and Toddlers by Kathleen Odean

Babies Need Books by Dorothy Butler

Board books with rhymes that focus on specific famous painters written by Julie Merberg and Suzanne Bober:

Dancing With Degas

Painting With Picasso

How Is Mona Lisa Feeling?

In The Garden with Van Gogh

Sharing With Renoir

On An Island With Gauguin

A Picnic With Monet

Quiet Time With Cassatt

A Magical Day With Matisse

Animals In Art: Art From The Start

Sunday With Seurat

Ballet With Degas

Texture Books To Read And Feel:

Trucks by Debbie Powell

Millie Moo (Funny Friends) by Roger Priddy

Marley Springs Ahead by John Grogan

Charlie Monkey (Funny Friends) by Roger
    Priddy

Hoppity Hop Peekaboo by Dawn Sirett

Fuzzy Fuzzy Fuzzy by Sandra Boynton

Dinosaur's Binkit by Sandra Boynton

Baby Faces Peekaboo! by Dawn Sirett

Who Do You Love? by Martin Waddell

Touch and Feel: Pets by Dorling Kindersly

Touch and Feel: Wild Animals by Dorling
  Kindersly

John Deere: Touch and Feel: Tractor by
  Dorling Kindersley

That's Not My Puppy by Fiona Watt

That's Not My Train by Fiona Watt

That's Not My Dinosaur by Fiona Watt

Touch and Feel: Fire Engine by Dorling
  Kindersley

Touch and Feel: Farm by Dorling Kindersley

Touch and Feel: Playtime by Dorling
  Kindersley

I Want To Be A Builder by Andrea
  Pimmington

COMING SOON

Coming in May 2013.....

Busy Toddler, Happy Mom: New Discoveries
and Skills Using Sensory Bins

Sign Up for the Busy Toddler, Happy Mom
Newsletter at busytoddlerhappymom.com to
receive more Toddler Activities and Updates
on New Books.

ABOUT THE AUTHORS

Gayle Jervis has been writing curriculum ever since she taught English at a public school. She participated in starting a new course called Perspectives For Living and much of what she wrote was taken province wide to help other new teachers teach this course. When Gayle and her husband began their own family, she began writing curriculum for her own young children. When she decided to home school, her curriculum writing increased as she needed to find ways to teach two children who had two very different learning styles. During this time, she became involved in a local home school association and she became their librarian determined to build up their resources to help other home school parents. She also published a monthly newsletter for its members. Later, she became president of the association and during those two years, she hosted a large provincial home school conference. Now as her children have started their own families, she has begun once again to write appropriate curriculum especially for her two toddler grandchildren. It is her heart's desire to help moms of young toddler to harness the energy of their little people and to develop those necessary skills to prepare them for preschool.

Kristen Jervis Cacka graduated from university in business with the intention of starting her own business. However, she changed her plans when she met her husband and instead she has been enjoying staying at home with her lovely daughter. Therefore, as Kristen began looking for appropriate materials for her young toddler, she became frustrated by the lack of fun curriculum that could be used in a home setting. That was when she and her mom, Gayle, decided to collaborate their talents and create a series of books not only meeting her goals for her own daughter but helping other moms looking for similar activities.

12752785R00099

Made in the USA
San Bernardino, CA
25 June 2014